Write Charlie
An incredible journey in pictures

Designed by Harry Thompson

Edited and with a foreword by Reg Thompson

Profits from the sales of this book go to support Child Bereavement UK

Front Cover: Charlie's name written with light sticks using time-lapse photography on a beach at night in Fiji.
Sent by Ben from Tribewanted.

First published in Great Britain in 2017 by Reg Thompson.

12 Davidson Close,
Gt. Cornard
Sudbury
Suffolk
Co10 oyu

ISBN : 978-1-5272-1652-5

Publisher : Reg Thompson
Design : Harry Thompson

Original website F2B; now, Green Duck:
http://www.greenduck.co.uk/

Printed and bound by Lavenham Press (2017)

Lavenham Press Limited, Arbons House
47 Water Street, Lavenham, Suffolk CO10 9RN

info@lavenhamgroup.co.uk

Over the following 120 pages you will find photographs taken in more than 60 countries over a period of nearly twelve years. All of the photographs have one thing in common; they feature my daughter Charlie's name. The idea for this book began in the spring of 2006, nearly five months after Charlie died in a train accident at Elsenham station in Essex.

Charlie was only thirteen years old. She was at the beginning of her life and like so many other young people of a similar age, she was full of excitement and emotion, eager to experience new things and to discover the world. She was a child of great tenderness and compassion. Moved to tears by a news report on famine in Africa, she proclaimed loudly that she would volunteer as soon as she was old enough, and go to Africa and help people less fortunate than herself. She was equally passionate about animals. Once, riding home on our bicycles from a trip to the shops, she spotted a wounded pigeon in a bank of stinging nettles. Directing me from her bicycle saddle, she coordinated the rescue operation and within half an hour and a hundred nettle stings later, I passed the injured pigeon into her safe hands. Toby (all rescued animals received names immediately) stayed with us for three weeks until his or her wing healed and then spent some time sitting on the roof before flying off, probably never to be seen again.

In the weeks and months after her death, our family struggled to survive. Wrapped in shock and disbelief, days dissolved into one another and any future seemed bleak and hopeless. We were supported by friends and family, rarely left alone, and then in April of 2006, we received a letter with a photograph inside. It was from a friend who had lived nearby when the children were young and who had always made Charlie and her two brothers very welcome in her house. It was a photograph of Charlie's name written in stones in the Gobi desert. It did not take us long to come up with the idea for WriteCharlie. With the help of a supportive local tech company, a website was created and later, a Facebook page. We spread the word and asked anybody we knew who was going on holiday, to spend a few minutes writing Charlie's name and asking them to send the photograph to the website. Back in 2006, I wrote on the site that one day we hoped to publish a book of photographs for charity. Now, nearly twelve years later, that wish has come true.

Charlie has travelled to so many exotic places but also and more importantly into the hearts and minds of hundreds of people; friends, family and complete strangers. It is true to say that these photographs have done much to sustain us over the years. They have proven to us that people, all around the world, are united in love and that life continues to have meaning long after we ourselves are gone. This book exists because of these people.

Mongolia, Gobi desert, Autumn 2006, taken by Di Nicholson

This was our first picture. The one that started Charlie on her journey

EUROPE

NORTH
AMERICA

Atlantic
Ocean

ASIA

Pacific
Ocean

AFRICA

SOUTH
AMERICA

OCEANIA

Indian
Ocean

This map shows where photographs
of Charlie's name have been taken
all around the world. From Iceland
to Australia and from Alaska to the
Antarctic, people have written
Charlie's name in sand, with stones
and deck chairs, in semaphore and
with skis. They have written her
name on simple notes in
extraordinary places, even under
water, and once with elephant dung!

ANTARCTICA

Alaska, Mendenhall Glacier, Juneau, 2007
Taken by Heather Holt

Alaska

'Charlie in Alaska' 2007, taken by Carol

Somewhere in Antarctica, Autumn 2006
Taken by James Nicholson

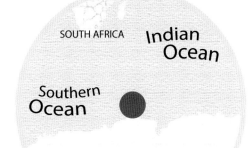

Antarctica

Argentina, Bariloche 2007, The Gough brothers, struggling for oxygen half way up a mountain in The Andes, manage to create Charlie's name out of skis and the imaginative use of their own bodies. Fortunately neither brother found himself frozen in that position for too long.

Santiago

Buenos Ares

ARGENTINA

CHILE

South Atlantic Ocean

Moreno Glaciers

Argentina, Moreno glacier near El Calafate 11 December 2007, taken by Tobias Freestone. In Patagonia, it is the only glacier in the world which is growing and is made from compressed snow rather than ice.

Secluded beach near Mandurah, Perth, 2008
Taken by Amanda Strathearn

WESTERN AUSTRALIA

● Perth

Australia

Melbourne
January 2007
Clare Mcpartland
scratched Charlie's name
on some
bamboo
so she
wouldn't
get lost in
a bamboo forest.

QUEENSLAND

NORTHERN

TERRITORY

● Melbourne

**Melbourne
Cricket Ground, 2007
Taken by Melanie Nimmo**

Louisa Creek, Mackay, Queensland 7 May 2007
Taken by Jonathan Tolhurst

Australia

Australia, Paul Herron took this picture on the beach at Cairns in Australia. He has a heart bigger than Queensland. March 2013

QUEENSLAND
Cairns
Townsville

Australia, a fabulous photograph from Emma in Australia. Charlie at Uluru. It is a place of enormous spiritual significance to the aboriginal people. October 2017

Sydney, 5 October
2007, taken by
Russell Jameson

Australia

Bahamas

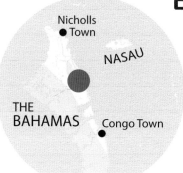

On the beach, April 2007, taken by Julian Cinque

Persian Gulf

Bahrain

SAUDI ARABIA

BAHRAIN

Duba

QATAR

● Riyadh

UNITED ARAB EMIRATES

'Charlie, Kingdom of Bahrain'
Thuwaiba holding an arabic script, 2008, taken by Wendy Fieldhouse with Thuwaiba's kind permission.

OMAN

Red Sea

YEMEN

Bolivia

CUBA

MEXICO

NICARAGUA

Salt Flats, 23 November 2007
Taken by Tobias Freestone, slightly
concerned, having thrown out his water
bottle to make room for the play blocks he
needed to write Charlie's name.

Brazilian Rainforest, April 2007
Taken by Paul Pink

PERU

BRAZIL

BOLIVIA

ARGENTINA   PARAGUAY

Brazil

Rio de Janeiro, Charlie on Sugarloaf mountain and at Igauazu Falls, 'the Devils' throat', marking the border between and Brazil, Autumn 2007

Brazil

BRAZIL

Rio de Janeiro

São Paulo

Porto Alegre

Argentina
Taken by Mark Cook

Cambodia
Phnom Penh
July 2007
Taken by
Matt & Tracey

CHALIE

THAILAND
LAOS
Bangkok
CAMBODIA
VIETNAM
Ho
Chi Minh City
Gulf of
Thailand

ALASKA

Charlie on Whistler Mountain in British Columbia, July 2007, taken by Philip Loader. Charlie's name is held by Scott, Jenny and Suzie Loader. The location became the base for the 2010 winter Olympics some 120 kms north of Vancouver.

Lake Louise, Alberta, Canada 2007, taken by Kirsty Stroud

British Columbia

Alberta

● Edmonton

● Calgary

Vancouver

Canada

U.S.A

Canada

From the the observation level, 342 m (1,122 ft) high, at the top of the CN Tower in Toronto. April 2008, taken by Doug White

Shells on the beach, Lanzarote June 2007 Taken by Jonathan Davies and Family

Canary Islands

Chile

Chile, January 2008, taken by Maureen Walbaum

BOLIVIA

CHILE   PARAGUAY

ARGENTINA

URUGUAY

South
Pacific Ocean

The Andes, 2007
'Very high up'
Taken by
Rose Benson.
I don't
know how
she did this
without making
any footprints?

21

China

Tiger Leaping Gorge on the Yangtze River
May 2008, taken by Tobias Freestone

Croatia, Summer 2008,
Charlie spelt out in Flag
Semaphore, taken by Billy

Prague, Charles Bridge, Czech Republic, 29 April 2007, taken by Kath, family and friends, Kearsley, Bolton

GERMANY POLAND

CZECHIA

Munich

AUSTRIA

Sailing around the Croatian Islands, Summer 2007, taken by Michael Green

Dominican Republic

Dominican Republic
June 2007, taken by Paula Harding and Family

Croatian Islands

The Nile at Aswan,
April 2007, Taken by Viv Foulkes-Arnold

Naama Bay beach, Sharm El Sheik, October 2007
Taken by Ann McElhoney

Egypt

Egypt, Under the Red Sea, 2007, taken by Ann McElhoney at the site of the wreck of the SS Dunraven which foundered on a reef on the 25th of April 1876 en route from Bombay to Liverpool.

Charlie pointing the way at Land's End in the summer of 2007. Created and taken by Abigail Thurgood-Buss.

Charlie the tawny owl, named by the Raptor Foundation at St Ives, 2007, taken by Doug White

England

England

Norwich ●

Southwold Beach in Suffolk
September 2008
Taken by
Edward
Pearce

Southwold ●

Cambridge ●

Chrishall, July 2007
Taken by Olivia Wallace

Chrishall ●

Colchester ●

Point Clear beach, Clacton, 7 July 2008, taken by Sarah & Miles

Castlerigg Stone Circle, near Keswick, the Lake District, August 2007, taken by Paul and Mel Bowe

England

England, Dovestone reservoir, Peak District 2007, taken by Jackie Smith and Keith Philbin

31

England

Stonehenge

Salisbury

London

Charlie

Stonehenge, 17 June 2007, taken by Anne and
Steve Bell

Brighton, 2007, taken by Linda Johnstone

Brighton

English Channel

England

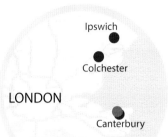

Ipswich
Colchester
LONDON
Canterbury

Wind chime in an apple tree, Cornwall,
April 2007, taken by Marie Hulme

Daisies in Whitstable, 2007, taken by Jen Hughes

England, Widdington Walkers Club - High Crag, Buttermere, Lake District
28 April 2007, taken by Paul Hearn and Matt

Charlie at Chelsea Football Club, Stamford Bridge, **London**
October 2007, taken and created by Billy Burgoyne

England, Charlie graffiti in North London, July 2007, painted by Robbie & Harriet Griffey

England

Little Walden, 5 September 2016, taken by Hayley Martin, "Wow it's windy today and I couldn't help but think of Charlie, she dances in the wind, the straw was getting blown everywhere and its not the best but here's to you Charlie!"

Overlooking the fields on the edge of Chard, May 2007, taken by Carol Schipper and Jenny Barnes

Little Walden

London

Chard

England

Clovelly, Devon, 15 July 2008, taken by Linzi Taylor who was one of Charlie's best friends.

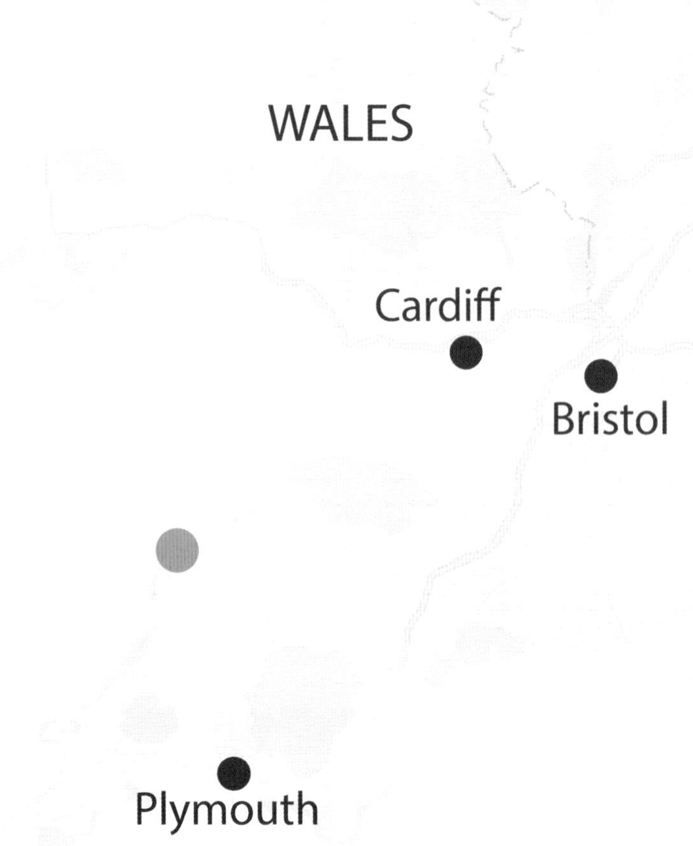

WALES

Cardiff

Bristol

Plymouth

A beautiful photograph from Beth Meader. Gulf Rocks, Holywell Bay, near Newquay in Cornwall. Beth and Charlie once went there together. Today Charlie was there again, carried safely in Beth's heart.

Newquay

Holywell Bay

Penwith Heritage Coast

Falmouth

England

gh Town

England, Nikki Jordan sent me this picture. It was taken on the hilly fields behind the Institute in Colchester. Charlie's name is made up by all the students of the Film and Television class of 2009. They gave it to me on the day they graduated. I didn't even know they knew about Charlie. There was nothing they could have done that could have meant more to me.

London, We wrote Charlie's name ourselves this afternoon in Gerard and Maria's back garden somewhere off the Holloway Road. It was Linda's idea and a huge host of O'sullivans made it possible. Ethan who is 9 and a better photgrapher than me, took the picture while standing on the garden wall. Charlie would have loved it.

The year ten pupils from Newport Free Grammar School spell out Charlie and Liv's names on the playing fields. Richard Bland took the photograph standing thirty feet up on the platform of a Cherry-Picker, kindly provided by the local Fire Brigade.

England, July 2007, taken by Richard Bland

Pupils of Saffron Walden County High School, Essex, England, May 2007, taken by Rob Loe

This photograph was presented to me at the end of my first ever week of teaching. We lived near Saffron Walden and I had just signed up to take a PGCE. It was the summer of 2007, about eighteen months after the accident. Rob Loe, who was head of English and Film Studies at the school, took a huge chance and arranged for me to deliver a series of lectures to the sixth form. I can remember feeling sick with nerves, but what I remember most vividly was how friendly and interested the students were. I didn't know they knew about Charlie but, I suppose, living in or around Saffron Walden, it would have been hard for them not to know. They presented me with the photograph after the last lecture. I think I cried.
They hadn't known Charlie but they cared.

England

Falkland Islands, Gypsy Cove, Christmas 2006, taken by Sergeant Mick Owen. The penguins were just passing by. They did not offer any help at all.

ARGENTINA

CHILE

FALKLAND ISLANDS

Distance: 9,129.85 miles (14,693.07 km)

FINLAND

**Charlie's name in a Finnish forest
2007, taken by Gudrun**

**Schoolchildren in Mali, Fiji 2007, taken by Paul
Simpson**

FIJI

Fiji

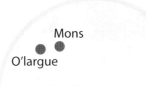

Mons

O'largue

Béziers

Narbonne

**Olargues, south of France,
August 2007, taken by Robbie Thompson**

**Harry remembers Charlie even though he is
standing in a hole, next to the Tarrassac bridge,
near Mons, France, August 2012
Taken by Peter McPartland**

France

France

Charlie in Paris
25 April 2007
Taken by
Marc
and
Dee

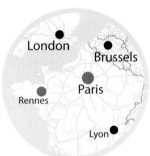

Camelias
One of the traditional flowers of Brittany, June 2007, taken by Francoise Tricard near Rennes

48

Galapagos, San Cristobal Island on Puerto Chino beach taken by Drou. Now Charlie is going to places that I didn't even know existed. Thank you Drou.

Germany

Charlie

In the German North Sea,
In memory of
Charlie and Jenny
2008
Taken by
Uwe Boken

A typical field in Spring
April 2007, taken by Amalyna Azman

Ghana, this is by courtesy of the children of Kumasi Children's Home in Ghana and also by courtesy of Mel Dane who volunteered in Ghana to work with and help children.

Greece, West coast of the Peloponnese near Patras, the leaves used were from the different trees in the area, floating on a swimming pool at dusk. This picture was submitted with no name.

Greek island of Halki,
2007, taken by Rachael Goor

Hawaii

Seaweed Charlie
Hawaii 2007, taken by Lou Godden

Greece

53

Holland

CHARLIE

Batavia in Lelystad, The Netherlands, 2007

SWEDEN

Copenhagen

DENMARK

Somewhere in the middle of the North Sea, July 2007, taken by Beck Bowe

ENGLAND

THE NETHERLANDS

London

BELGIUM

GERMANY

POLA

Iceland, Heimaey, Westman Islands, 2007, taken by Dave Owen

India, Palolem Beach, South Goa
5 September 2016, taken by Matilda Finch Darling

India, dental and medical instruments create Charlie's name, 2007, taken by Will Gough

INDIA
Arabian Sea · Bay of Bengal
SRI LANKA

India

Taj Mahal, Agra, 21 April 2008, taken by Tobias Freestone who scored a respectable eleven points with this picture

CHINA

INDIA

INDONESIA

Indian Ocean

5:30am on Mount Kinabalu, 4095 metres/13,000 feet, April 20 2008, taken by Alison Dolphin

Indonesia

Croagh Patrick, Count Mayo, April 2007
Taken by Richard Bland

Wexford
2007, taken by
Susan Kemp

Ireland

59

Israel, Dead Sea, 10 August 2007
Taken by Emma Fredskild Green

CROATIA

BOSNIA &
HERZEGOVINA

**Mount Etna, 9 September 2007
Taken by Sanny and Gio**

MONTENEGRO

● Rome

ITALY

Mount Etna
Sicily ●

Mediterranean Sea

Italy

JRKEY

Italy, The Colosseum, Rome
2007 Taken by Charles Harris

Kenya, some of the team at Turtle Bay Beach Club, Nyari, 2007, taken by Caroline Rowsell

Kenya

Nyari or Hells Kitchen,
September 2007, taken by Caroline Rowsell

**On the Beach, April 2007
Taken by Octavia and
Luke Barnett**

Lanzarote

Malawi, sunset over Lake Malawi
June 2008, taken by Nicky Carter

Malaysia, Outside the Petronas Towers in Kuala Lumpur, 26 February 2008, taken by Tobias Freestone

Nepal, taken by Karen Noble 2017

New Zealand, it looks pretty treacherous. It is the glacier on Mount Cook in the South Island. The sort of place Charlie would definitely have insisted on visiting if we had ever gone to New Zealand. It was taken by a friend of Caitlin Phillips Diggons. Thank you Caitlin and thank you to Caitlin's friend. It is wonderful.

New Zealand
Lake Wanaka in the middle of South Island, 10 Jauary 2008, taken by Tobias Freestone

Tom and Abbi Welham wrote Charlie's name on the beach at White Silica Sands in the very far north of New Zealand on their recent fantastic holiday. Thanks guys. It's fantastic.

New Zealand

Auckland

Hot Water Lakes

Wellington

Mount Cook

Lake Wanaka

Dunedin

Hot Water Lakes extinct volcano 2007 Taken by John Unsworth

New Zealand, Tongariro National Park, 30 December 2007, taken by Tobias Freestone. Mount Ngahuru in the background (Mount Doom)

New Zealand

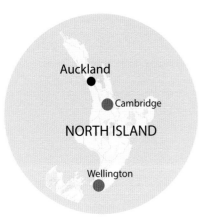

Flowers, Wellington, April 2007, taken by Hazel

Cambridge, North Island, January 2008, taken by John Unsworth

New Zealand, another picture by a friend of Caitlin Phillips Diggons. A glacier on Mount Cook in the South Island. Thank you Caitlin and thank you to Caitlin's friend.

Oman, Beach, March 2007
Taken by Tobias Freestone

Machu Picchu, Autumn 2007
Taken by Mark Cook

ECUADOR

BRAZIL

● Lima District

● ● Cusco

BOLIVIA

South Pacific
Ocean

Peru

Peru, Machu Picchu,
Cusco, November 2007,
Taken by Toby and Laura

Portugal

Sao Rafael beach
Algarve 2007, taken by Jill Freestone

Gdynia-Orlowo 2007
Taken by Anita & Tomek Klas

Poland

Scotland, the Isle of Bute, somewhere on the west coast of Scotland seconds before a blizzard swept in from the Atlantic. Thank you Hazel, it is utterly beautiful. March 2013

Singapore, Concert Hall
2007, taken by John Unsworth

Singapore, Sri Veeramakaliamman temple
March 2007, taken by Richard O'Sullivan

MALAYSIA

SINGAPORE

Singapore Straight

Batam

The Sultan Mosque
March 2007, taken by Ina Ibrahim

Singapore

CHARLIE

Solomon Islands
2007, Taken by Kezzie

South Africa, near Cape Town, Summer 2007. Taken by the pupils of Newport Free Grammar.

South Africa, Cape Town
Cape Point, where the Atlantic
and Indian Ocean meet. 15 June
2008, taken by Tobias Freestone

NAMIBIA   BOTSWANA   MOZAMBIQUE

Pretoria

Johannesburg   SWAZILAND

Hermanus Restaurant, Capetown, April 2007
Taken by Kiaran Milligan

LESOTHO   Durban

Durban,
July 2007,
taken by
Angie and
Tayla Powell

South Africa

Cape Town

On the Spanish border with Portugal, in 'wolf country', April 2007, taken by Di Nicholson

Spain

Sagrada Familia, Bercelona
October 2007, taken by Krys and Keith Bather

South of Spain, 2008, taken by Melanie Nimmo

Posada del Peine, Madrid 2007, taken by Katie

Spain

Spain

FRANCE

Lyon

Bay of Biscay

Bordeaux

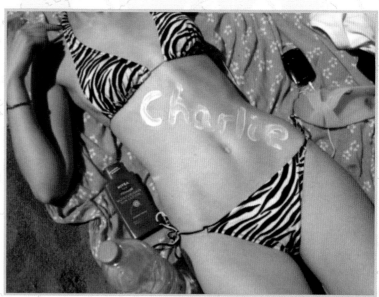

'Sunscreen Charlie' in Barcelona, June 2007
Taken by Alice van Hees

Barcelona, June 2007, taken by Alice van Hees

SPAIN

Balearic Sea

Barcelona

Spain, Almeria
2007, taken by Siany

89

Sri Lanka

A beach in Sri Lanka
2007, taken by Emily Nicholson

Alcúdia, Majorca, 18 June 2007
Taken by Jeff Nicks

Spain

Sri Lanka

Karen Noble has
worked her magic
and Charlie finds herself
on this breath-taking
beach in Sri Lanka

Sweden

DENMARK
SWEDEN
Copenhagen ● ●
Malmö

GERMANY

**Malmö
Sweden
2007, taken by
Klaus Fredlander
Close to the
"Oeresundsbridge"
linking
Sweden
and
Denmark**

Taiwan

RUSSIA

MONGOLIA

NORTH KOREA

SOUTH KOREA

JAPAN

Tokyo

Shanghai

CHINA

Hong Kong

TAIWAN

PHILIPPINES

Taiwan, 2007
The Black bearded Barbarian,
George Leslie Mackay,
who dedicated his life to
bringing medical and
spiritual succour to the
people of Taiwan.
Taken by Yalin Huang

Tanzania, Uhuru Peak, the summit of Kilimanjaro
23 July 2008, taken by Rosalind Smith
At 19,335ft/5895m this is the highest point in Africa

Tanzania, the summit of Mount Kilimanjaro from Lisa who is a friend of Sara Thom who I last saw about twenty years ago. Thank you both so much

Tanzania, Maasai tribe in Arusha, 23 July 2007, taken by Stephanie Lord while working on a Voluntary Development Education project

Thailand

Tunisia

Tunisia 2007, taken by Tiffany,
a close school friend

The picture was sent by Georgia Murray.
"My friend Jack went to Thailand and i
told him about the Write Charlies Name Charity
and he came back with this picture…xxxxxx"

Turkey, Caretta Beach, Dalyan
May 2007, taken by Louise Wright

Istanbul

Izmir TURKEY

CYPRUS

Mediterrean Sea

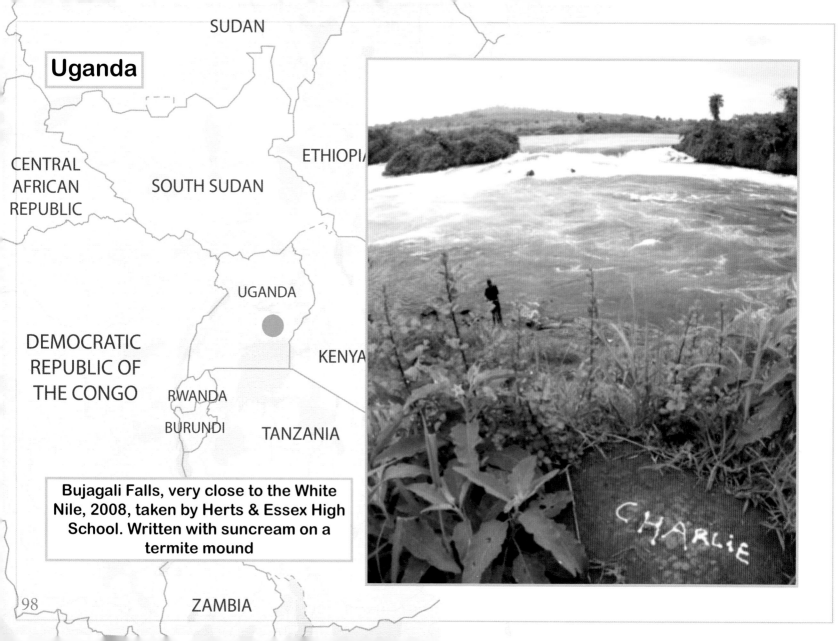

Uganda

Bujagali Falls, very close to the White Nile, 2008, taken by Herts & Essex High School. Written with suncream on a termite mound

Golden Gate Bridge, USA, June 2007, taken by Linzi Taylor

St Sophia Cathedral, Kiev 2007, taken by Alison Dolphin

Ukraine

USA

USA

Las Vegas, USA, September 2007
Taken by Monique & Janice Nelson

Hoover Dam, USA,
September 2007
Taken by Monique
& Janice Nelson

USA, Victorville, California, 2007, taken by Paul Spencer. These aircraft were parked here after the terrorist attacks of September 11, 2001, because airlines could no longer afford to keep so many flights in the air, and because hangars at many US airports were full.

ANDREW KENT
JAMES McGEE · JOSEPH KERR · GEORGE KIMBLE
JAMES NOWLAN · ROBERT McKINNEY · EDWARD
CLELLAND KINLOCH SIMMONS · GEORGE PAGAN · CHRISTOPHER
JOHN W THOMSON · ANDREW DUVALT
JOHN M THRUSTON

CHARLIE

Charlie,
a hero in her own right,
with the Heroes of the Alamo,
Austin, Texas, USA 2007.
Taken by
Carol Schipper

CANADA

USA

WASHINGTON MONTANA NORTH DAK

OREGON IDAHO WYOMING SOUTH DAKOTA

NEBRAS

NEVADA UTAH COLORADO KAN

CALIFORNIA NEW OKL

ARIZONA MEXICO TEXAS

MEXICO

Pacific Ocean

USA

ARIZONA

Grand Canyon National Park

Navajo Nation Reserve

Pheonix

Tuscon

MEXICO

**Grand Canyon
September 2007
Taken by Monique & Janice Nelson**

**Tucson, Arizona, June 2007, taken by
Jennifer Serrano**

USA, Grand Canyon Arizona, May 2007 taken by Clive and Margeret Ingram

USA

Charlie in letters twenty feet high on Myrtle Beach in South Carolina. Thank you Linda. If Charlie had been writing her own name, this is how she would have done it.

USA

Tampa Bay,
Florida, 2007,
Taken by
E.V.F. Poulter.
The Parrot played
no part in writing
Charlie's name, it
just barged in.

Jacksonville

Orlando

Tampa

Miami

USA, The White Sands National Monument, Alamogordo, New Mexico, September 2008, taken by Claire & Mark, "It was scorching hot, but the sand was so pure and white, it looked like snow."

USA, FedEx Stadium, Washington DC, taken by James Gough, home of the Washington Redskins who were playing the Pittsburg Steelers.

CANADA

Niagra Falls

New York

Philadelphia

Baltimore

Washington

**Times Square,
New York
2007, taken by Lynn Blake**

 Richmond

USA, Niagara Falls
2007, taken by Carol

Charlie

110

Vietnam, Miu Ne, Summer 2008, taken by Helena Bland

LAOS
CAMBODIA VIETNAM
Ho Chi Min South China Sea

Wales

The Great Orme
Llandudno, North Wales, July 2007, taken by Ali Dolphin in memory of Charlie and Sophie.

Llanfairfechan with Puffin Island in the background, Wales, 27 August 2007
Taken by Llinos Thomas

Zambia, 2007, Charlie's name created out of elephant dung with considerable care by Diana Rocktail.

Zimbabwe, Andy Lines enlists some willing help on the great Zambezi river. Another extraordinary destination on Charlie's journey. Thank you Andy and Andy's friend

This book is dedicated to the memory of Charlie Thompson
and to all the children who have gone too soon

Dan Thompson
Jamie Thompson
Liv Bazlinton
Milena Gagic

Your light will never dim.

If you want to write Charlie's name she still has many countries to visit.
www.writecharlie.org

This book was made possible by these 121 people

David Rozalla

Tim Greenard

Leanne Gagic

Kate Dane

Lydia Scott

Zoe James

Sam James

Olivia Grace Bere

Greg Whittle

Bob Nochol

Joe Fleetwood

Carl Stickley

Dan Gough

Madeleine Budd

Ryan Everett

Lily-Anne Clarke

Demi Johnson

Laura Yapp

Patrick Freestone

Harry Genge

Bridie Harris

Lewis Wright

Michael John Toogood

Liz Smith

Nicola Sessions

Maria Watson

Maggi Rose

Claire Haines-Clarke

Marian Johnson

Sue Norris

Christina Hughes

Cath Brandley

Richard O'Sullivan

Rita Wood

Richenda Devereux

Suzanne Wood

Charles

Alex Andrews

Kiefer

Emma

Liz Goodall

Joanne and Lee Bradley

Jayne Folkard

The Gardner Family

Patricia Pritchard

Wendy Bell

Nicky withycombe

Sue Richardson

Mandy

Matthew Morgan-Stevens

Michelle Marple

Amanda Watts

Jackie Jones

Lucy Crofton

Sam King

David and Patricia Thompson

Billy Phillips-Diggons

Tom TX Welham

Michelle & Dave

Adam Andrews

Danielle Wrayton

David Cleaver

Sandy Greenard

Matthew McGuchan

Mark Carne

Barbara Sweeting

David Howkins

Melanie Carter

Amanda Marshall

Matilda Finch Darling

Ruby Hollis

Linda O'Sullivan

Kate Mccoid

Phil Brown

James Coppin

Oli Freestone

Julie Robins

Mike Claydon

Toby Freestone

Jenny Willans

Steven Jack Lee-taylor	Kate Hurst
Helen Fewell	Bridget Gough
Jenny Kilgannon	Carole Manners
Michelle Marriott	Judith Toogood
Jo Pallett	Valerie Pink
Sue Williams	Ian
Judy Stanton	Sam Timmins
Will Grantham	Sara Thom
Elaine McLaren	Russell Jamesen
Kyle Leslie	Lorna and Simon
Lizzy Ellam (Pop Fury)	Tiffany
Andy Lines	Clare Barker
The Wiggetts	Catherine Ives
Joe Philpott	Robyn Dane

Richard Bland

Ann Currie

Linzi Shelford

Clare McPartland

Steve and Amanda

Emily Nicholson

Vicky Blackwell

Carl Alan Hooper

Andrea Owen

Harriet Griffey

Christina Hughes

Diana Nicholson

Jack Williams

Janet Edwards

Francesca Maria Johnston